TAYLOR SWIFT'S ERAS TOUR
in a nutshell

*A Billion-Dollar Spectacle That Celebrated
the Evolution of a Pop Superstar*

Felix Grayson

MINDSPARK
PUBLISHING

For the seekers of simplicity, the curious minds who crave the essentials without the fluff—this one's for you. Here's the story, in a nutshell.

"Brevity is the soul of wit."

— *William Shakespeare*

"Simplicity is the ultimate sophistication."

— *Leonardo da Vinci*

"Any fool can make something complicated. It takes a genius to make it simple."

— *Woody Guthrie*

IN A NUTSHELL'S PURPOSE

To provide quick, engaging overviews of pop culture, history, and trending topics, making it easy for readers to get the gist of any story.

IN A NUTSHELL'S MISSION

To deliver concise, entertaining content that educates and satisfies the curiosity of our readers and listeners in an ever-changing world of popular culture.

IN A NUTSHELL'S VISION

To be the go-to source for quick, digestible insights on the people, events, and trends shaping our world.

IN A NUTSHELL'S CORE VALUES

Simplicity: Making information clear, concise, and accessible.

Curiosity: Encouraging exploration and learning about diverse topics.

Entertainment: Providing facts in a fun and engaging way.

Timeliness: Keeping up with current events and trends.

CONTENTS

INTRODUCTION

In 2023, the world witnessed an extraordinary musical event: Taylor Swift's Eras Tour. This tour was not just another series of concerts; it was a multi-dimensional journey through Swift's evolution as an artist, a storyteller, and a cultural icon. With each performance, she took her audience on a captivating voyage through her distinct musical eras, from the country-inspired ballads of her youth to the introspective and experimental sounds of her more recent works. The Eras Tour quickly became a cultural phenomenon, redefining what a concert could be and leaving a lasting impact on music, fashion, social media, and fan communities around the globe.

This book aims to capture the essence of the Eras

Tour, exploring the artistry, business acumen, and profound cultural influence that made it a billion-dollar spectacle. From the electrifying opening night to the tour's emotional conclusion, "Taylor Swift's Eras Tour in a Nutshell" delves into the meticulous planning, creative storytelling, and fan engagement that set this tour apart. It celebrates Swift's legacy as an artist who has not only transformed her music but also used her platform to inspire and connect with millions.

Taylor Swift's journey through her various musical phases has been marked by bold reinvention and personal growth. Each era, with its distinct sound, aesthetic, and narrative, has resonated with fans in unique ways, reflecting the complexities of life, love, and self-discovery. The Eras Tour was an homage to this evolution, an immersive experience that allowed fans to relive the moments that defined Swift's career and, by extension, their own lives. The tour was not just about the music; it was about the shared memories, emotions, and growth that come with embracing each phase of one's journey.

As you explore the pages of this book, you will

journey through the planning and execution of the Eras Tour, the fan culture that fueled its success, and the social and economic impact it had around the world. We'll reflect on how this tour redefined the concert experience, setting new standards for artists everywhere, while also highlighting the powerful message of change, resilience, and self-celebration that Swift imparted through her performances.

"Taylor Swift's Eras Tour in a Nutshell" is more than just a chronicle of a groundbreaking tour; it is a tribute to the artistry, innovation, and human connection that music can inspire. Whether you are a devoted Swiftie or simply intrigued by the spectacle of a billion-dollar concert, this book invites you to relive the magic of the Eras Tour and to celebrate the transformative power of music.

CHAPTER 1: SETTING THE STAGE – THE JOURNEY TO THE ERAS TOUR

From Country to Pop – The Early Eras

Taylor Swift's journey began in the heart of country music. With her self-titled debut album in 2006, a teenage Swift introduced the world to her storytelling prowess, combining raw emotion with relatable lyrics. Songs like "Tim McGraw" and "Teardrops on My Guitar" resonated with young listeners and country music fans, marking the arrival of a fresh voice in the industry. Swift's ability to weave tales of love, heartbreak, and youthful experiences through her lyrics quickly set her apart.

Swift's subsequent albums, "Fearless" (2008) and "Speak Now" (2010), cemented her status as a country music sensation. "Fearless" saw her honing her songwriting craft, with hits like "Love Story" and "You Belong With Me" crossing over to mainstream pop charts. These songs not only expanded her fanbase but also began blurring the lines between country and pop genres. By the time "Speak Now" was released, Swift was known for her deeply personal songwriting style, making her a voice for a generation navigating the complexities of young love and growing up.

The pivotal shift came with her 2014 album "1989." Swift's first full-blown foray into pop music, "1989" was a bold departure from her country roots. The album's sound was influenced by 80s synth-pop, and hits like "Shake It Off" and "Blank Space" showcased a new, confident, and playful side of Swift. The album's success was monumental, marking Swift as a global pop icon. "1989" not only brought her a new wave of fans but also positioned her as a musical chameleon who could effortlessly adapt to different styles while maintaining her signature storytelling.

Reputation and Reinvention

By 2017, Taylor Swift had become a household name, but her journey to the "Reputation" era was not without challenges. The years leading up to "Reputation" were marked by public scrutiny, high-profile feuds, and media controversies. Swift was often portrayed as a "good girl" in the media, but her narrative began to change with public disputes involving celebrities and the constant spotlight on her personal life. The scrutiny took a toll, leading Swift to reinvent her image and sound.

"Reputation" was Swift's response to the storm of criticism and drama surrounding her. The album marked a drastic shift both in tone and aesthetics. With darker, edgier visuals and lyrics that confronted her critics, Swift embraced a new persona that was unapologetically bold. Songs like "Look What You Made Me Do" and "...Ready for It?" showcased this defiant attitude, while tracks like "Delicate" revealed a vulnerability beneath the tough exterior.

The "Reputation" era represented a turning point for Swift. It allowed her to reclaim her narrative, transforming public perception and demonstrating her resilience. The era was a reminder that Swift was not just a pop princess; she was an artist capable of evolving, facing controversies head-on, and using them as fuel for her creative expression. This reinvention set the stage for Swift's next phase, where she would once again pivot and surprise the world with her multifaceted artistry.

A Return to Roots – Lover, Folklore, and Evermore

After the stormy "Reputation" era, Taylor Swift embarked on a path of self-reflection and renewal with her 2019 album, "Lover." This album marked a return to a more vibrant and hopeful sound, embracing themes of love, self-acceptance, and joy. With "Lover," Swift shed the darkness of "Reputation," opting for pastel colors and whimsical visuals. Songs like "Lover," "You Need to Calm Down," and "ME!" embodied a more lighthearted and introspective side of Swift, emphasizing themes of love and positivity. It was a celebration of who she had become, both as an artist and as a person.

The unexpected turn came in 2020 when Swift released "Folklore" and later "Evermore," two albums that showcased her introspective storytelling in an entirely new musical context. With these albums, Swift pivoted to a more alternative and indie-folk sound, drawing inspiration from isolation and introspection during the global pandemic. "Folklore" was rich with narrative-driven lyrics, weaving stories of fictional characters and reflective themes. Tracks like "Cardigan" and "Exile" presented a mature, stripped-down version of Swift's songwriting.

"Evermore," described as a "sister album" to "Folklore," continued this exploration of moody, folk-inspired music. Together, these albums were a testament to Swift's creative versatility, highlighting her ability to delve deep into different musical landscapes while staying true to her storytelling roots. These projects not only garnered critical acclaim but also expanded her audience. This period of musical experimentation laid the groundwork for the Eras Tour, where Swift could revisit and celebrate every phase of her artistic journey.

The Concept of Eras – Crafting a Unique Tour

The idea of the "Eras Tour" emerged as a natural extension of Swift's diverse discography. Swift has always been a master of reinvention, each album marking a distinct phase in her life and career. By structuring the tour around these different "eras," Swift created a concept that would allow her to take fans on a journey through her musical evolution. It was an ambitious project, aiming to showcase not just individual albums, but the entire spectrum of her artistry.

The tour's concept was unique in that it didn't focus solely on promoting a new album. Instead, it was a retrospective celebration of Swift's entire career. From her country roots to her pop anthems and introspective ballads, the Eras Tour aimed to highlight the defining moments and musical milestones of her journey. Each "era" would be brought to life on stage with meticulously crafted set designs, costumes, and visual elements that encapsulated the essence of each album.

By choosing this structure, Swift emphasized that her music was more than just songs; it was a narrative that evolved with time. The Eras Tour would give fans an opportunity to relive the highs and lows, the nostalgia, and the growth that characterized Swift's career. This concept of celebrating all of her past and present selves resonated with fans, adding an element of storytelling to the tour that was both personal and universal.

Building Anticipation – Teasers and Announcements

With the concept of the Eras Tour taking shape, the next step was to build anticipation. Swift has always been a master of creating buzz around her projects, and the lead-up to the Eras Tour was no different. She began dropping hints and teasers on social media, sparking excitement among her fanbase. From cryptic posts to subtle references to her past albums, Swift engaged her audience in a game of speculation, making the tour announcement an event in itself.

The official announcement of the Eras Tour was met with a frenzy of excitement. Swift utilized multiple platforms, including Instagram and Twitter, to share promotional images and messages that hinted at the tour's multi-era theme. Her team also released promotional videos and behind-the-scenes glimpses into the tour's preparation, keeping fans on the edge of their seats. This strategy not only generated hype but also created a sense of involvement, making fans feel like they were part of the journey.

Swift's engagement with her audience extended

beyond traditional promotion. She interacted with fans online, acknowledged their excitement, and even responded to fan theories, further fueling anticipation. This level of interaction made the Eras Tour feel personal and inclusive, a celebration not just of Swift's career but of the community that supported her throughout the years.

CHAPTER 2: BEHIND THE SCENES – PLANNING A BILLION-DOLLAR TOUR

Creative Process – Designing the Show

Designing the Eras Tour was an exercise in creativity, innovation, and meticulous planning. For Taylor Swift, this tour was more than a concert series—it was a narrative journey through her musical evolution. The creative process began with a vision: to celebrate every distinct phase of her career in one cohesive show. Swift, known for her hands-on approach, took an active role in every step of this process, from storyboarding to selecting songs that best captured the spirit of each "era."

Swift's team started by creating a narrative arc for the concert, deciding how to transition between each era seamlessly while maintaining the unique vibe of each album. Storyboarding was crucial in this stage, with Swift and her creative directors mapping out each segment of the show. They aimed to take the audience on a journey that reflected Swift's artistic growth, beginning with her country roots and progressing through her pop, indie-folk, and introspective phases.

Song selection was another key aspect. Swift has an extensive discography, so narrowing down the setlist was no easy task. She needed to balance fan-favorite hits with deeper cuts that captured the essence of each era. This required careful curation, ensuring that the setlist flowed naturally from one era to the next. Swift also wanted to surprise fans, so she incorporated acoustic versions and rearrangements of her songs to keep the performances fresh and un-predictable.

Visual storytelling played a crucial role in de-signing the show. Swift's team conceptualized elaborate stage designs, lighting, and visual effects for each era. For instance, the "Reputa-tion" segment demanded darker, edgier visuals, while "Lover" needed vibrant, pastel aesthet-ics. Swift also integrated costume changes and choreography that matched the mood of each musical phase, further enhancing the audience's experience. The creative process was, therefore, an interplay of music, visuals, and performance art, all meticulously crafted to showcase the dynamic evolution of Swift's career.

Production and Logistics – Making It All Happen

Turning the creative vision of the Eras Tour into reality required a monumental logistical effort. The production team faced the challenge of creating a show that was not only grand in scale but also versatile enough to adapt to different venues around the world. Each concert had to be a seamless experience for thousands of fans, involving a vast array of elements like stage design, lighting, sound, special effects, and pyrotechnics.

Stage design was the backbone of the tour's logistics. The production team designed an expansive, multi-level stage that could accommodate various sets representing each musical era. This included movable parts, platforms, and intricate props that were all integrated into a carefully choreographed performance. Given the show's elaborate nature, the stage had to be adaptable for different stadiums and arenas, requiring engineers to create a modular design that could be assembled and disassembled efficiently.

Lighting and sound were crucial to creating the show's atmosphere. The lighting design had to change dynamically to reflect the mood of each era, from the soft, golden hues of "Fearless" to the bold, neon lights of "1989." Sound engineers worked meticulously to ensure that Swift's voice and music were balanced, regardless of the venue's acoustics. They also incorporated immersive sound effects to enhance the story-telling aspect of the performance.

Special effects were the final layer in bringing the Eras Tour to life. Swift's team employed cutting-edge technology, including high-definition screens for visual projections, laser light shows, and pyrotechnics that punctuated key moments of the concert. Swift's use of pyrotechnics and confetti cannons during specific songs became signature moments that fans eagerly anticipated. Every detail, down to the timing of the sparks and the bursts of color, was orchestrated to create a sense of magic and wonder.

The logistical complexity of the tour extended beyond the performances. Swift's team managed a fleet of trucks to transport the equipment and stage sets across cities, coordinated with local crews for setup and teardown, and maintained a strict schedule to keep the tour running smoothly. The sheer scale of production highlighted the ambition and dedication behind making the Eras Tour a spectacular experience.

Team Swift – The Collaborators

Behind Taylor Swift's captivating performances was an army of collaborators who helped realize the Eras Tour's vision. Swift handpicked a team of industry professionals, each bringing expertise in various aspects of production. From choreographers and musicians to designers and technical crews, "Team Swift" was a well-oiled machine that worked tirelessly to bring the show to life.

The choreographers played a vital role in crafting the dynamic movements and dance sequences that defined each era. Swift worked closely with her choreographers to ensure that the dance routines reflected the mood of the songs and enhanced the overall storytelling. They created routines that ranged from high-energy pop numbers to more subdued, emotive dances for her folk-inspired tracks. These choreographed elements were not just background entertainment; they were an integral part of the narrative Swift aimed to convey.

Musical directors and the band were equally instrumental. Swift's live band needed to be versatile, capable of switching genres seamlessly throughout the show. They reimagined some of Swift's songs to fit the live performance context, adding unique instrumental solos and arrangements that elevated the concert experience. Swift's musicians were an extension of her artistry, bringing a level of spontaneity and freshness to each performance.

Designers also played a crucial role, particularly in costume and stage design. Swift's costumes for the tour were meticulously planned to align with each era's aesthetic. Working with top fashion designers, Swift curated outfits that embodied the essence of her albums—from sparkly bodysuits for "1989" to whimsical, bohemian dresses for "Folklore." These costumes not only enhanced the visual spectacle but also provided fans with iconic fashion moments.

Technical experts, including lighting engineers, sound technicians, and visual effects coordinators, were behind the seamless execution of the show. Their expertise ensured that every light cue, sound mix, and visual projection worked in harmony to create an immersive experience for the audience. Together, these collaborators formed the backbone of the tour, making Swift's artistic vision a reality on the world stage.

Merchandising and Marketing

The Eras Tour's success was not limited to ticket sales; merchandise and marketing were pivotal components of its billion-dollar status. Swift's team developed an extensive merchandise line that reflected the themes and aesthetics of each era. This included clothing, accessories, posters, and collectible items, all designed to resonate with fans and serve as mementos of the tour experience.

One of the standout elements was the era-specific merchandise. Fans could purchase items themed around their favorite album, such as t-shirts emblazoned with "Fearless" lyrics, "1989" bomber jackets, or "Folklore" hoodies. This personalized approach allowed fans to express their connection to Swift's various musical phases. Additionally, limited-edition items were released periodically, creating a sense of exclusivity and urgency that drove sales.

Swift's marketing strategy was equally savvy. The tour was promoted through a multi-channel approach, using social media, traditional advertising, and word-of-mouth buzz generated by Swifties. Swift and her team released promotional videos and behind-the-scenes glimpses that teased the tour's production, building anticipation among fans. Social media played a critical role, with Swift using platforms like Instagram and TikTok to engage directly with her audience, share updates, and create viral moments.

Partnerships with brands also added a layer of commercial success. The tour's sponsors and collaborators were carefully chosen to align with Swift's image and the tour's themes. These partnerships extended beyond traditional advertising, involving exclusive merchandise drops and special fan experiences. The strategic blend of merchandising and marketing not only amplified the tour's visibility but also created additional revenue streams, contributing significantly to the tour's billion-dollar valuation.

Economic Planning – Managing a Billion-Dollar Budget

Executing a tour on the scale of the Eras Tour required astute economic planning. Swift's management team approached the tour with a clear financial strategy, balancing artistic ambition with practical considerations. Budgeting for a tour of this magnitude involved accounting for production costs, travel expenses, marketing, staffing, and more, all while ensuring profitability.

Ticket pricing was a critical component of the tour's financial strategy. Swift's team employed dynamic pricing models, adjusting ticket prices based on demand to maximize revenue. Despite controversies over high ticket prices and swift sell-outs, this approach helped the tour achieve record-breaking sales. Swift also worked to provide a range of ticket options, including VIP packages that offered exclusive merchandise and experiences, catering to different segments of her fanbase.

Managing expenses was another key focus. The production team optimized logistics to ensure that the tour could move efficiently from one city to another, minimizing costs without compromising the quality of the show. This involved detailed coordination of transportation, venue setup, and local staffing, requiring a balance between speed, safety, and cost-effectiveness.

Strategic partnerships with sponsors and brands provided additional financial backing, offsetting some of the production costs. These partnerships often involved cross-promotional opportunities, allowing sponsors to benefit from the tour's vast reach while providing Swift with supplementary income. By carefully managing the budget and exploring multiple revenue streams, Swift's team turned the Eras Tour into a financial juggernaut, setting new standards for concert tours worldwide.

CHAPTER 3: KICKING OFF THE ERAS TOUR – THE OPENING NIGHT

The Buzz – Building Hype for Opening Night

In the weeks leading up to the Eras Tour's opening night, anticipation reached a fever pitch. Taylor Swift and her team expertly orchestrated a marketing campaign that fueled excitement among fans and the media alike. Social media became a battleground of speculation as Swifties dissected every teaser, cryptic post, and subtle hint Swift dropped. The hype was palpable, and each new piece of information about the tour—be it a new promotional image, rehearsal clip, or cryptic countdown—added to the growing buzz.

Swift's approach to building anticipation was a masterclass in fan engagement. She began by releasing a series of cryptic social media posts, each alluding to different "eras" of her career. Fans quickly picked up on these clues, launching into full-scale investigations, sharing their theories across platforms like Twitter, TikTok, and Instagram. Swift encouraged this speculation, occasionally liking posts or leaving comments, which sent fans into a frenzy and kept the momentum building.

Media outlets also joined in, speculating about the tour's setlist, production scale, and potential surprises. Headlines focused on Swift's return to the concert stage, with many dubbing it one of the most anticipated tours of the decade. Interviews with insiders revealed tantalizing details about costume changes, set designs, and choreography, adding to the mounting excitement. The narrative of the Eras Tour as a career-spanning celebration dominated the conversation, setting the stage for an unforgettable opening night.

The final countdown saw Swift drop hints about possible surprises, further stoking fan excitement. As the opening night approached, ticket holders took to social media to share their preparations—crafting friendship bracelets, planning concert outfits inspired by Swift's eras, and organizing travel plans. The tour had already become a global phenomenon before a single note was sung, and the world eagerly awaited its grand debut.

The Opening Act – Setting the Tone

As fans began to fill the venue on opening night, the atmosphere was electric. Concert-goers, dressed in outfits representing their favorite Taylor Swift eras, added to the vibrant, communal feel of the event. The venue was buzzing with excitement as fans exchanged friendship bracelets, a tradition inspired by Swift's lyrics and the camaraderie within the Swiftie community. The stage itself, hidden behind a massive curtain, teased the grandeur that lay in store.

The pre-show vibe was a mix of nervous anticipation and sheer exhilaration. Opening acts had been carefully chosen to complement Swift's music, setting the tone for the multi-era journey that would unfold. The crowd erupted as the first opening act took the stage, kicking off the night's festivities. These performances were energetic, designed to pump up the audience while providing a taste of the diverse musical influences that defined Swift's own evolution.

Between acts, the venue lights dimmed, and the stage crew began to make final preparations. Massive LED screens around the venue displayed a countdown, heightening the tension. Fans chanted, held up signs, and waved glow sticks in the air, creating a sea of lights and colors. Every minute that passed brought the crowd closer to the main event. The sheer scale of the production was evident in the intricate details visible even from the farthest seats—giant screens, pyrotechnics setups, and the sound of final mic checks hinted at the spectacle that was about to begin.

As the countdown reached its final seconds, the crowd's energy peaked. The lights dimmed completely, plunging the venue into darkness, followed by a collective gasp. Then, the first notes played, and the curtain lifted, revealing a stage transformed into a magical world. The tone was set, and the audience knew they were about to witness something extraordinary.

A Night to Remember – The Concert Experience

The opening night of the Eras Tour was nothing short of a spectacle. As the curtain rose, Taylor Swift emerged amidst a dazzling light show, greeted by deafening cheers. She began the concert with a high-energy performance that instantly captivated the audience. Swift chose to kick off the night with a song from her "Fearless" era, signaling the start of a journey through her musical evolution. Fans sang along word-for-word, their voices blending with Swift's in a powerful display of collective nostalgia.

The concert was structured like a narrative, with each "era" presented as a distinct chapter in Swift's career. Swift guided the audience through her discography, from the twang of her country roots to the synth-pop beats of "1989," the edginess of "Reputation," and the folk-inspired melodies of "Folklore" and "Evermore." The transitions between these eras were seamless, with each segment featuring its own set design, costumes, and visual effects. The stage transformed before the audience's eyes, moving from golden fields to neon cityscapes and forested groves, each representing the mood and aesthetic of the respective era.

The setlist was a carefully curated blend of hits and fan favorites. Swift interspersed high-energy anthems like "Shake It Off" and "Look What You Made Me Do" with more intimate acoustic performances of tracks like "All Too Well" and "Cardigan." These quieter moments allowed for raw, emotional connections, as Swift shared personal anecdotes and expressed gratitude to her fans. It was during these performances that the audience's collective silence spoke volumes, hanging on to every note and word.

Notable moments from the opening night included surprise elements, like Swift's unannounced duet with a special guest, much to the crowd's delight. The concert's climax arrived in the final era, where pyrotechnics lit up the stage in a dazzling display, culminating in a standing ovation as Swift took her final bow. It was an experience fans would carry with them, a memory etched in their hearts as they exited the venue, still buzzing from the adrenaline of the night.

Swift's On-Stage Presence

Taylor Swift's stage presence on the opening night was magnetic. She moved effortlessly across the stage, commanding attention with each step, yet exuding an air of humility and approachability. Swift's ability to connect with her audience was palpable; she treated the vast stadium as an intimate gathering, making eye contact with fans, acknowledging their signs, and responding to their cheers.

Swift's charisma shone through in her interactions between songs. She shared stories behind her lyrics, reminisced about the early days of her career, and spoke openly about the journey that had led to this moment. These candid moments created a sense of closeness, as if Swift were having a personal conversation with each person in the audience. The crowd responded with cheers, laughter, and even tears, fully engaged in the experience.

Her vocal performance was another highlight. Swift delivered each song with a blend of technical skill and raw emotion, adapting her vocal style to match the tone of each era. During the more upbeat numbers, she was energetic, dancing with abandon and playfully interacting with her backup dancers and band. In the ballads, her voice softened, drawing the audience in with its vulnerability.

Swift also displayed an impressive level of

stamina and focus throughout the multi-hour concert. Despite the complexity of the show — with its numerous costume changes, choreography, and special effects—Swift navigated it all with grace, never missing a beat. Her on-stage presence was a testament to her professionalism, passion for her craft, and deep appreciation for the fans who made the journey worthwhile.

Immediate Impact – The Aftermath

The impact of the opening night was immediate and far-reaching. As the concert ended, fans flooded social media with photos, videos, and reactions, creating a digital tidal wave of buzz. Hashtags related to the Eras Tour trended worldwide, with clips of Swift's performances and interactions quickly going viral. Fans shared their concert experiences, from the goosebumps during "Enchanted" to the joy of exchanging friendship bracelets. The online conversation was a celebration of Swift's artistry, the tour's production value, and the sheer emotional rollercoaster of the night.

Media outlets published rave reviews, praising Swift's ability to craft a tour that was both a retrospective of her career and a spectacle in its own right. Critics highlighted the concert's ambitious scale, the seamless blending of different musical styles, and Swift's electric stage presence. Articles and broadcasts dissected the opening night, from setlist choices to costume designs, further cementing the Eras Tour's place in pop culture.

The opening night's success set a high bar for the rest of the tour. It established the Eras Tour as not just a series of concerts, but as a cultural event that encapsulated Taylor Swift's evolution as an artist. Swift's performance on the first night left fans eager for more, with tickets for future dates selling out even faster in the wake of the buzz. The concert's aftermath solidified Swift's reputation as a master performer and storyteller, leaving both fans and the music industry in awe of what she had accomplished.

CHAPTER 4: THE ERAS – A CELEBRATION OF MUSICAL EVOLUTION

The Fearless Era – Nostalgia and Youth

The Eras Tour's celebration of the "Fearless" era was a nostalgic tribute to Taylor Swift's early days in country music. This segment of the concert brought the audience back to a time when Swift, with her signature curls and acoustic guitar, sang about young love, heartbreak, and the bittersweetness of growing up. The set design and visuals evoked a sense of innocence and warmth, transporting fans to the late 2000s when Swift first captured their hearts.

Swift opened the "Fearless" segment with fan favorites like "Love Story" and "You Belong With Me." These songs, with their timeless tales of romance and longing, resonated with the crowd, many of whom had grown up listening to Swift's early hits. The staging for this era was designed to evoke nostalgia, featuring golden hues, fairy-tale elements, and country-inspired motifs. Swift herself wore outfits reminiscent of her early tour costumes, complete with flowy dresses and cowboy boots, paying homage to her country roots.

The energy in the stadium was electric as Swift

and her band performed the tracks with a mix of the original country twang and a modern twist. The crowd sang along to every word, their voices merging with Swift's in a chorus of collective memory. This segment was more than just a performance; it was a celebration of youth, dreams, and the simple yet profound emotions that characterized Swift's early songwriting.

Swift's narration between songs added depth to the experience. She shared anecdotes from her early career, reflecting on the innocence and ambition that drove her as a young artist. These moments connected with fans on a personal level, as Swift spoke about the journey from the small-town girl strumming a guitar to the global superstar standing before them. The "Fearless" segment of the tour reminded everyone of the joy and vulnerability of youth, laying the foundation for the evolution that followed.

The Pop Breakthrough – 1989 and Beyond

The transition to the "1989" era marked a significant shift in tone, highlighting Taylor Swift's groundbreaking leap into the pop music scene.

This segment was infused with high-energy performances, neon lights, and a vibrant, cityscape-inspired set design that captured the album's modern, sleek aesthetic. Swift's transformation into a pop icon was evident as she strutted across the stage in glittering outfits, backed by a troupe of dancers that amplified the era's upbeat, carefree vibe.

Kicking off with the album's smash hit, "Shake It Off," Swift brought a sense of liberation and celebration to the stadium. The song's infectious energy spread like wildfire through the crowd, with everyone dancing and singing along. "Blank Space" and "Style" followed, each performance showcasing Swift's ability to craft pop anthems that were both lyrically sharp and sonically catchy. The choreography and visuals during this segment were dynamic, with screens projecting futuristic graphics and vibrant colors that encapsulated the album's bold, confident spirit.

Swift's vocal delivery in this era was strikingly different from her country roots. She embraced a more polished, synthesized sound while maintaining the emotive quality that defined her music. The contrast between the "1989" era and earlier segments of the concert highlighted her evolution as an artist willing to take risks and explore new musical territories. Swift engaged with the audience, inviting them to let go of their worries and dance through the songs that had become anthems of self-empowerment.

The "1989" segment also included a nod to Swift's later pop works, seamlessly blending tracks like "Delicate" and "Getaway Car" from "Reputation." This blending of eras emphasized Swift's pop breakthrough as a continuous journey, showcasing her ability to adapt and thrive within the ever-changing landscape of mainstream music. The exhilarating, unapologetically pop atmosphere of this segment captured the essence of Swift's musical metamorphosis, leaving the audience in awe of her versatility.

The Dark and Bold – Reputation

When the lights dimmed and a heavy bassline began to reverberate through the stadium, the atmosphere shifted to a darker, edgier tone, signaling the arrival of the "Reputation" era. This segment of the concert was a masterclass in theatrical performance, with Swift adopting a bolder persona that was both empowering and confrontational. The stage transformed into a dystopian wonderland, complete with towering LED screens displaying moody visuals, smoke machines, and lightning effects that mirrored the album's themes of defiance and self-reclamation.

Swift kicked off the "Reputation" era with the fierce track "...Ready for It?" Her commanding presence and intense choreography captivated the audience, who responded with raucous cheers. Swift wore sleek, black costumes adorned with glittering details, embodying the rebellious spirit of the album. Each song in this segment, from "Look What You Made Me Do" to "Don't Blame Me," was delivered with a mix of attitude and vulnerability, reflecting the complexities of Swift's public persona during this period of her life.

The performances were punctuated by powerful visuals, such as images of snakes—a symbol Swift had reclaimed during the "Reputation" era—slithering across the screens. These visuals reinforced the narrative of the album, which dealt with themes of reinvention, resilience, and the reclamation of one's story. Swift's stage interactions during this segment were more assertive, with moments where she stared defiantly into the camera, underscoring her message of self-empowerment.

Despite the era's darker undertones, there were moments of vulnerability that reminded fans of Swift's multifaceted nature. During "Delicate," the mood softened, and Swift's vocals conveyed a sense of honesty and introspection, bridging the gap between the boldness of "Reputation" and the emotional storytelling of her subsequent albums. This era showcased Swift's ability to confront her fears and challenges head-on, transforming them into powerful art that resonated with fans worldwide.

The Personal Revival – Lover, Folklore, and Evermore

The atmosphere took a turn toward the whimsical and introspective as Swift transitioned into the "Lover," "Folklore," and "Evermore" segments. These performances marked a return to a more personal, heartfelt sound, showcasing Swift's evolution into a mature artist exploring themes of love, loss, and self-reflection. The stage was bathed in soft, pastel colors for "Lover," while "Folklore" and "Evermore" brought in earthy, woodland-inspired visuals that evoked a sense of intimacy and tranquility.

During the "Lover" segment, Swift donned pastel-colored outfits and performed songs like "Lover" and "You Need to Calm Down" with a sense of joy and tenderness. The crowd swayed to the dreamy melodies, caught up in the romantic and self-assured atmosphere of the album. Swift's interaction with the audience here was warm and inviting, often smiling and gesturing to fans, creating a sense of community within the stadium.

The "Folklore" and "Evermore" eras offered a more subdued, storytelling experience. Swift traded her high-energy dance routines for an acoustic guitar and piano, delivering stripped-down versions of tracks like "Cardigan" and "Willow." These moments felt almost like an intimate fireside concert, with Swift weaving tales of fictional characters and personal reflections. The stage design for these segments was lush and organic, featuring faux forest backdrops and dim, warm lighting that created an atmosphere of quiet contemplation.

This segment highlighted Swift's growth as a songwriter and storyteller. Her vocals were raw and emotive, conveying the depth and nuance of her more recent works. The audience was visibly moved, many holding up lights and swaying gently as they absorbed the lyrics. These performances emphasized Swift's ability to pivot from pop anthems to soulful ballads, reinforcing her status as a multifaceted artist who could touch on universal emotions with grace and authenticity.

Bringing It All Together – A Multi-Era Celebration

The final act of the Eras Tour brought all of Swift's musical phases together in a breathtaking celebration of her journey. This segment served as a testament to Swift's evolution as an artist, blending the diverse sounds, themes, and aesthetics of each era into a cohesive narrative. The stage came alive with an explosion of colors, lights, and visuals, representing the culmination of Swift's career and the legacy she had built.

Swift moved seamlessly between songs from different eras, demonstrating how her music, though varied in style, shared a common thread of storytelling and emotional resonance. The setlist was crafted to highlight this narrative, juxtaposing tracks like "Love Story" with "Cardigan" to show the progression from youthful romance to mature introspection. The audience, fully immersed in the experience, sang along to every word, celebrating not just the music but the memories associated with each era.

The concert's grand finale featured a medley of hits from across Swift's discography, accompanied by an array of fireworks, confetti, and visual effects that filled the stadium with a sense of magic and triumph. Swift took center stage, addressing the crowd with heartfelt gratitude and reflecting on the journey they had shared. Her closing words encapsulated the spirit of the Eras Tour: a celebration of growth, change, and the enduring power of music.

As the final notes played and the lights dimmed, the audience erupted into applause, their cheers echoing through the stadium. The tour had not just celebrated Swift's musical evolution; it had reaffirmed the connection between her and her fans, a bond forged through the stories and emotions captured in each era. The Eras Tour was, in every sense, a multi-era celebration of artistry, resilience, and the transformative power of music.

CHAPTER 5: THE SWIFTIES – THE HEART OF THE TOUR

Swifties Unite – Fan Culture and Community

The Eras Tour was not just a celebration of Taylor Swift's musical journey; it was a testament to the passion and dedication of her fans, affectionately known as the "Swifties." This global community of fans played a crucial role in the tour's success, creating an atmosphere that extended far beyond the concert venues. Swifties, bound together by their love for Swift's music, formed a vibrant subculture that came to life in full force during the Eras Tour.

From the moment the tour was announced, Swifties united online and offline, organizing fan meet-ups, creating fan art, and sharing their excitement across social media platforms. Twitter, Instagram, TikTok, and dedicated fan forums buzzed with activity, as fans speculated about setlists, outfits, and potential surprises. The Eras Tour became a shared experience that connected people of all ages and backgrounds, transforming the Swiftie fandom into a global movement.

The Swiftie community is known for its creativity and camaraderie. They create art, fanfiction, and covers of Swift's songs, using platforms like YouTube, TikTok, and Instagram to showcase their talents. For the Eras Tour, Swifties took this creativity to new heights. They designed outfits inspired by Swift's different eras, crafted elaborate signs for concerts, and even organized friendship bracelet exchanges. The fandom's enthusiasm and willingness to support one another reflected the values Swift has embodied throughout her career: kindness, inclusivity, and self-expression.

The sense of community among Swifties extended into the concert experience. Fans traveled from around the world to attend the tour, turning the concerts into epic gatherings where strangers became friends through their shared love for Swift's music. This unity and mutual support made the Eras Tour feel less like a series of isolated events and more like a collective celebration of art, growth, and resilience.

Concert Rituals – Friendship Bracelets and More

Swifties brought a unique set of traditions and

rituals to the Eras Tour, adding layers of meaning and fun to the concert experience. One of the most heartwarming rituals was the exchanging of friendship bracelets, inspired by Swift's lyrics from the song "You're On Your Own, Kid." In the weeks leading up to the tour, fans crafted bracelets with beads and charms, often including lyrics, song titles, and inside jokes related to Swift's music. At the concerts, Swifties swapped these bracelets with fellow fans, creating moments of connection and shared joy.

The bracelet exchange became a phenomenon in itself. Swifties shared stories of these exchanges on social media, highlighting the friendships formed and the sense of community they experienced. Some fans even prepared hundreds of bracelets to distribute, each one representing a tiny piece of Swiftie love and camaraderie. This ritual transformed the concerts into spaces of kindness, where fans celebrated not just Swift's music, but also the relationships and bonds that it had helped foster.

Dressing up for the concert was another cherished tradition. Swifties drew inspiration from Swift's different musical eras, crafting elaborate outfits that reflected the aesthetics of albums like "Fearless," "1989," and "Lover." The concert venues became fashion shows, filled with sequined dresses, cowboy boots, glittering bodysuits, and pastel ensembles. Fans reveled in the creativity of their outfits, often referencing iconic Swift looks or lyrics. This act of dressing up was more than just fun; it was a way for fans to express their connection to specific periods of Swift's career and to celebrate the personal significance her music held for them.

Fans also brought signs to the concerts, each with messages ranging from witty puns to heartfelt declarations. Some signs were meant to capture Swift's attention, while others simply expressed admiration and gratitude. These traditions enriched the concert atmosphere, turning each event into a festival of fan culture, where every attendee played a part in creating the magic of the Eras Tour.

Swift's Fan Engagement – Making Every Show Special

Taylor Swift's connection with her fans has always been at the heart of her success, and the

Eras Tour was no exception. Swift made every concert feel personal, going out of her way to interact with fans and make each show unique. She took notice of fan signs, acknowledged their enthusiasm, and even shared personal stories that resonated with the audience. These interactions created a sense of intimacy, despite the massive scale of the venues, making every fan feel seen and appreciated.

One of the most beloved aspects of the tour was the inclusion of "surprise songs" in each concert. Swifties eagerly awaited this segment, where Swift would perform a different song not on the setlist, chosen spontaneously each night. Fans speculated endlessly about which songs might make an appearance, creating an element of surprise that added to the excitement of attending the concert. Swift introduced these songs with stories and anecdotes, explaining their significance and her reasons for choosing them, further deepening the connection with her audience.

Swift also took time during each show to express her gratitude to the fans. She spoke about their role in her journey, acknowledging how their support had carried her through the ups and downs of her career. These moments of sincerity resonated deeply with the crowd, often moving fans to tears. Swift's speeches highlighted the reciprocal relationship between artist and fan, turning the concerts into more than just performances—they were heartfelt celebrations of a shared journey.

Beyond the stage, Swift engaged with fans online, liking posts, leaving comments, and occasionally sharing fan content on her own platforms. This digital interaction extended the concert experience, allowing Swift to connect with fans who couldn't attend in person. By engaging so directly with her audience, Swift reinforced the sense that the Eras Tour was as much about the fans as it was about her music.

Viral Moments – Social Media's Role

The Eras Tour was a social media sensation, with fans documenting every aspect of the experience and sharing it across platforms like Tik-Tok, Instagram, and Twitter. From concert outfit reveals to emotional reactions during surprise songs, Swifties generated a continuous stream of content that amplified the tour's visibility. Hashtags related to the tour trended regularly, and clips from concerts quickly went viral, spreading the excitement beyond the concert venues to Swift's global fanbase.

One of the most viral aspects of the tour was the sharing of surprise song performances. Fans posted videos of Swift's live renditions, capturing her emotional delivery and the crowd's reactions. These clips circulated widely, creating a sense of collective participation for fans who couldn't attend the concerts in person. Swifties used social media to speculate on future surprise songs, exchange concert tips, and celebrate the joy of experiencing the tour together.

The friendship bracelet exchange also became a viral phenomenon. Fans shared tutorials on how to make the bracelets, documented their bracelet swaps, and posted photos of their growing collections. These posts showcased the creativity and generosity of the Swiftie community, painting a picture of the Eras Tour as a space of inclusivity and shared happiness.

Swift herself contributed to the tour's online

presence by engaging with fan content. Her occasional likes and comments on fan posts sent the Swiftie community into a frenzy, fueling even more content creation. This cycle of engagement between Swift and her fans kept the Eras Tour at the forefront of social media conversations, turning it into a cultural event that transcended the concerts themselves.

The Swiftie Economy – Supporting the Tour

The passion of Swifties extended into economic impact, as their support for the Eras Tour generated significant financial activity. Fans invested in concert tickets, often paying premium prices to secure seats at the highly anticipated events. Swift's decision to offer various ticket options, including VIP packages, catered to different budget levels while maximizing revenue. The demand was so high that it led to a frenzy of ticket sales, with many concerts selling out within minutes of being announced.

Beyond ticket sales, the Swiftie economy flourished through the purchase of tour merchandise. Swift's team offered a wide range of items, from clothing and accessories to collectible posters and memorabilia. Fans eagerly lined up at concert venues and online stores to buy official merchandise, proudly sporting t-shirts, hoodies, and bracelets that showcased their favorite eras. This merchandise became both a fashion statement and a tangible memento of their concert experience.

Swifties also contributed to the local economies of the cities hosting the tour. Many fans traveled long distances to attend concerts, booking flights, hotels, and rental cars, and spending money on dining, shopping, and sightseeing. This influx of tourism provided an economic boost to cities, especially those hosting multiple concert dates. Local businesses, aware of the Swiftie influx, often tailored their offerings, creating Swift-themed menus, events, and products to cater to the fanbase.

The financial impact of Swifties was a testament to their dedication and support. The Eras Tour became not just a musical event, but an economic force, driven by a fan community willing to invest in their shared love for Taylor Swift's artistry. This level of fan engagement not only fueled the tour's success but also demonstrated the profound influence Swift and her music wielded across multiple facets of society.

CHAPTER 6: THE BUSINESS IMPACT – A RECORD-BREAKING TOUR

Ticket Sales – A Frenzy of Demand

The announcement of Taylor Swift's Eras Tour sent waves of excitement through her fanbase, and when tickets went on sale, the demand was nothing short of overwhelming. Swifties flocked to ticketing platforms in droves, crashing websites and setting off a frenzy that demonstrated the unmatched draw of Swift as a live performer. The scramble for tickets was unprecedented, with millions of fans attempting to secure seats, resulting in one of the most intense ticket sales events in concert history.

Swift's team employed a variety of sales strategies to manage this high demand. They introduced a tiered pricing system, offering various options from general admission to premium VIP packages that included exclusive merchandise and behind-the-scenes experiences. Despite these efforts, the rush for tickets led to some controversy. Due to the overwhelming demand, ticket prices soared on resale markets, often reaching exorbitant amounts. Fans expressed frustration over scalping and dynamic pricing models that made it difficult for many to afford tickets. The situation sparked widespread debate over the fairness of ticket distribution and pricing in the concert industry, placing a spotlight on the need for reforms.

Despite these challenges, the sheer volume of ticket sales was astounding. Swift's decision to host multiple shows in major cities allowed her to maximize attendance, with each concert selling out in record time. The tour's ticket sales alone generated hundreds of millions of dollars, setting a new standard for concert tours and highlighting Swift's unparalleled ability to draw massive crowds. The frenzy surrounding ticket availability only added to the tour's mystique, making each show a coveted experience.

The ticket sale phenomenon underscored Swift's influence in the music industry and her status as a live performance juggernaut. It also revealed the complexities of managing large-scale tours in the digital age, where fan demand and market dynamics intersect in ways that challenge traditional ticketing models. The Eras Tour not only set records for ticket sales but also sparked important conversations about accessibility, fair pricing, and the evolving landscape of live entertainment.

Merchandise and Revenue Streams

In addition to ticket sales, the Eras Tour generated substantial revenue through a variety of streams, most notably concert merchandise. Swift's team meticulously crafted a range of merchandise that reflected the themes of her different musical eras, offering fans an array of products to commemorate their concert experience. The merchandise included t-shirts, hoodies, hats, posters, and accessories, each designed with aesthetic elements that resonated with Swift's albums. These items became hot commodities, selling out quickly both at concert venues and through online stores.

The concert venues featured extensive merchandise booths, where fans lined up hours before the show to purchase exclusive tour items. The merchandise was more than just souvenirs; it was a way for fans to express their connection to Swift's music and their presence at the Eras Tour. The products often incorporated iconic lyrics, album artwork, and symbols associated with Swift's eras, transforming them into cherished collectibles.

Beyond physical merchandise, Swift capitalized on digital revenue streams as well. She released special digital content related to the tour, including behind-the-scenes videos, digital albums, and limited-edition downloads. Fans eagerly purchased these digital offerings, further boosting the tour's revenue. The strategic use of digital content not only expanded the tour's reach but also provided fans who couldn't attend the concerts in person with a way to participate in the tour experience.

Swift's brand partnerships also played a role in generating revenue. Collaborations with select companies led to the creation of exclusive products, from custom apparel to themed beverages. These partnerships were carefully chosen to align with Swift's image and the tour's narrative, ensuring that each collaboration felt authentic and appealing to her fanbase. The combined revenue from merchandise, digital content, and brand deals contributed significantly to the Eras Tour's financial success, showcasing Swift's acumen in leveraging multiple revenue streams to maximize profitability.

Economic Impact – A Boost for Host Cities

The Eras Tour's influence extended far beyond ticket sales and merchandise; it had a substantial economic impact on the cities that hosted its concerts. As Swifties traveled from various regions and countries to attend the shows, they brought with them a surge in tourism, filling hotels, restaurants, and local attractions. This influx of visitors provided a significant boost to the hospitality and service sectors in each city, with some venues reporting record occupancy rates during the concert weekends.

Local businesses eagerly embraced the tour, tailoring their offerings to appeal to Swift's fanbase. Hotels offered special packages for concertgoers, while restaurants crafted Swift-themed menus and drinks to attract fans. Retailers stocked up on Swift merchandise, creating pop-up shops and displays that celebrated the event. This wave of economic activity created a festive atmosphere, transforming each city into a mini-hub of Swift-related excitement.

In addition to tourism, the Eras Tour generated employment opportunities. The tour's production required a large workforce, from stagehands and sound technicians to security personnel and event staff. Local vendors, food trucks, and transport services also benefited from the concert crowds, providing services that supported the influx of attendees. The economic ripple effect of each concert was significant, contributing to local economies and highlighting the positive impact of large-scale entertainment events.

The tour's impact on host cities went beyond just financial gains. It created a sense of community, as local businesses and residents embraced the Swifties who arrived in droves. Swift's concerts became city-wide events, fostering goodwill and collaboration between fans, businesses, and local authorities. This aspect of the Eras Tour reinforced the notion that concerts are not just about music; they are cultural happenings that can leave a lasting impression on the places they visit.

New Industry Standards – Redefining the Touring Model

The Eras Tour set new benchmarks for the music and concert industry, redefining what a large-scale tour could achieve in terms of production value, fan engagement, and revenue generation. Swift's approach to the tour showcased an innovative blend of storytelling, branding, and business strategy, offering a blueprint for future artists and event organizers seeking to create similarly impactful tours.

One of the tour's key innovations was its narrative structure. By organizing the concert around the different "eras" of her career, Swift created a unique storytelling experience that distinguished the tour from traditional album-promoting concerts. This concept allowed for a multifaceted performance that resonated with fans on an emotional level, setting a standard for how concerts can evolve into immersive, theatrical events.

Swift's dynamic engagement with her fanbase throughout the tour also redefined artist-fan interaction. The surprise songs, personalized speeches, and direct online engagement created a sense of intimacy that deepened the fan experience, proving that large-scale concerts can still foster meaningful connections. This level of engagement is now seen as a new standard for artists looking to build loyal fan communities and enhance the value of live performances.

The tour's financial strategy, including its diverse revenue streams, provided a model for maximizing profitability in the modern music industry. Swift's use of merchandise, digital content, and brand partnerships exemplified how artists can leverage their brand to generate revenue beyond ticket sales. The tour's impact on ticketing practices, despite its controversies, also sparked industry-wide discussions about fair pricing, dynamic pricing models, and efforts to combat ticket scalping.

In essence, the Eras Tour challenged and expanded the possibilities of what a concert tour could be. It combined music, storytelling, commerce, and fan engagement in a way that redefined industry expectations, setting a high bar for future tours and leaving a lasting legacy on the concert landscape.

Financial Milestones – The Billion-Dollar Success

The Eras Tour quickly became a financial phenomenon, achieving milestones that placed it among the most profitable tours in music history. Swift's meticulous planning, combined with her devoted fanbase, propelled the tour's earnings to unprecedented heights. Ticket sales alone generated hundreds of millions of dollars, and the combined revenue from merchandise, digital content, and brand partnerships pushed the tour's total income toward the billion-dollar mark.

The tour shattered records in multiple categories. It became one of the fastest-selling tours, with tickets for many dates selling out within minutes of their release. Swift also broke venue attendance records, performing to packed stadiums with tens of thousands of fans at each concert. The tour's merchandise sales were equally staggering, with fans purchasing millions of dollars' worth of items both at venues and online.

Beyond the immediate revenue, the Eras Tour solidified Swift's position as one of the most successful and influential artists in the music industry. Its financial achievements underscored the power of a well-executed tour strategy, one that combined artistic vision with savvy business practices. The tour's billion-dollar status was not just a reflection of Swift's popularity but also a testament to her ability to create a live experience that resonated deeply with fans and transcended the traditional concert model.

As the Eras Tour came to a close, it left behind a legacy of financial and cultural impact. Its success provided a case study in how to navigate the complexities of the modern entertainment landscape, inspiring artists, producers, and industry professionals to rethink the potential of live performances. The tour's record-breaking financial milestones ensured its place in music history, highlighting Taylor Swift's role not only as a pop superstar but also as a visionary in the business of music.

CHAPTER 7: SOCIAL AND CULTURAL IMPACT – BEYOND THE MUSIC

The Cultural Phenomenon – Swift's Influence

The Eras Tour quickly evolved into more than just a series of concerts; it became a cultural phenomenon that permeated various aspects of society. Taylor Swift's influence extended beyond the music industry, shaping trends in fashion, language, and social media. As fans immersed themselves in the tour's narrative, they adopted elements of Swift's style and ethos, turning the Eras Tour into a widespread cultural movement.

One of the most visible impacts of the tour was on fashion. Fans attended the concerts dressed in outfits inspired by Swift's different musical eras, from the sparkly dresses of the "1989" era to the vintage aesthetics of "Folklore." This sartorial celebration spilled over into everyday life, with Swift-inspired clothing trends appearing in retail stores and on fashion blogs. Sequins, pastels, and bohemian styles became part of a wider Swiftie fashion statement, reflecting how the tour influenced public tastes and consumer culture.

Language and social media trends were also

heavily shaped by the Eras Tour. Phrases from Swift's lyrics and tour moments entered the everyday vocabulary of fans and even those outside her immediate audience. Online, Swifties flooded platforms like TikTok, Twitter, and Instagram with content related to the tour, creating a digital archive of their experiences. Hashtags, memes, and challenges centered around the tour went viral, amplifying its reach and embedding it into the cultural consciousness. The tour's presence on social media became so pervasive that even non-fans found themselves participating in the conversation, demonstrating the tour's wide-ranging influence.

Beyond fashion and language, the Eras Tour contributed to a broader cultural narrative of self-expression and personal growth. Swift's journey, chronicled through her music and the tour, resonated with fans who saw reflections of their own experiences in her evolution. The tour became a celebration of change, resilience, and the complexities of identity, encouraging fans to embrace their own multifaceted selves. This cultural impact reinforced Swift's status not just as a pop star, but as a generational icon whose influence transcended music.

Swift's Advocacy – Using the Platform

Taylor Swift has long been known for using her platform to speak out on important social issues, and the Eras Tour was no exception. Throughout the tour, Swift subtly wove messages of advocacy into her performances, speeches, and interactions with fans, raising awareness about topics such as mental health, equality, and LGBTQ+ rights. While the concerts were primarily a celebration of her musical journey, they also served as a vehicle for promoting positive change.

During the "Lover" segment of the concert, for instance, Swift incorporated themes of self-love and acceptance, emphasizing the importance of equality. The performance of songs like "You Need to Calm Down" celebrated the LGBTQ+ community, and Swift's accompanying speech encouraged fans to support one another and stand up for inclusivity. These moments were not only empowering for attendees but also highlighted Swift's ongoing commitment to using her influence for social advocacy.

Mental health was another issue that Swift addressed during the tour. In her candid speeches between songs, she often spoke about the challenges of navigating fame and the importance of seeking support during difficult times. By sharing her own experiences with vulnerability, Swift helped destigmatize conversations around mental health, encouraging fans to prioritize their well-being. This openness resonated deeply with her audience, many of whom found solace and inspiration in her words.

In addition to her on-stage advocacy, Swift partnered with organizations and initiatives that aligned with her values. She made donations to local charities in the cities she visited, drawing attention to causes related to education, disaster relief, and social justice. These actions underscored Swift's dedication to using her platform for more than just entertainment, positioning the Eras Tour as not only a musical event but also a catalyst for social change.

Media Coverage – The Tour in Headlines

From the moment the Eras Tour was announced, it dominated media coverage across the globe. Major news outlets, entertainment magazines, and music blogs followed every development, from ticket sales to the setlist reveals, painting the tour as one of the most significant musical events of the decade. Swift's star power and the tour's sheer scale made it a frequent topic in both mainstream and niche media, keeping it at the forefront of public attention.

Media coverage of the tour was overwhelmingly positive, with critics praising Swift's artistry, the tour's production value, and the emotional depth of the performances. Headlines often focused on the tour's narrative structure, highlighting how Swift brought her entire career to life on stage in a way that resonated with fans and showcased her evolution as an artist. Reviews lauded her vocal abilities, stage presence, and the seamless blending of different musical styles, solidifying her reputation as a live performance powerhouse.

In addition to concert reviews, media outlets covered the tour's cultural impact, exploring its influence on fashion, fan culture, and social media. They published in-depth analyses of the Swiftie community, examining how the tour had become a space for self-expression and connection. Articles also discussed the economic implications of the tour, shedding light on how it boosted local economies and set new standards for concert tours in terms of revenue generation.

Swift's advocacy efforts during the tour did not go unnoticed by the media. Her support for social causes, both on and off the stage, was widely reported, reinforcing her image as an artist who uses her platform responsibly. The extensive media attention not only amplified the tour's reach but also helped shape Swift's public image, presenting her as a multifaceted artist whose influence extended far beyond music. The consistent presence of the Eras Tour in headlines kept it in the public eye, contributing to its status as a defining cultural moment.

A Global Connection – Reaching Fans Worldwide

While the Eras Tour primarily took place in select cities, its impact was undeniably global. Swift's international fanbase, spanning continents and cultures, connected through a shared passion for her music and the tour experience. For fans who couldn't attend the concerts in person, social media and digital content became vital tools for participating in the celebration.

Fans from around the world shared their tour experiences online, posting videos, photos, and personal stories that created a sense of global community. Platforms like TikTok and Instagram became digital concert venues, where fans could watch clips of surprise songs, see outfit reveals, and exchange stories. This virtual engagement allowed Swifties across the globe to feel connected to the tour, fostering a sense of inclusivity and belonging within the fandom.

Swift and her team also made efforts to reach international fans by releasing official digital content. Concert footage, behind-the-scenes videos, and tour-related merchandise were made available online, giving fans a taste of the tour experience regardless of their location. This strategy not only expanded the tour's reach but also demonstrated Swift's understanding of the importance of connecting with her global audience.

The international fan reactions highlighted the tour's universal appeal. Swift's music, with its themes of love, heartbreak, self-discovery, and resilience, resonated with people from diverse backgrounds, creating a shared emotional experience that transcended language and borders. The Eras Tour underscored the power of music as a global unifier and solidified Swift's position as an artist who could connect with audiences worldwide on a deeply personal level.

The Legacy of Eras – Swift's Impact on Future Artists

As the Eras Tour unfolded, it became clear that its impact would extend far beyond the concert circuit. The tour set new standards for live performances, offering a blueprint for future artists and influencing the music industry's approach to large-scale tours. Swift's innovative blend of storytelling, branding, and fan engagement provided valuable lessons for artists seeking to create memorable, multi-dimensional concert experiences.

One of the tour's most significant legacies is its narrative structure. By organizing the concert around her different musical eras, Swift showed that concerts could be more than just a series of performances; they could be cohesive narratives that tell a story and engage audiences on a deeper level. This approach inspired artists to think creatively about how to present their discographies, encouraging them to explore thematic elements and visual storytelling in their tours.

The Eras Tour also demonstrated the importance of fan engagement in shaping the concert experience. Swift's direct interaction with her audience, both online and on stage, set a new standard for how artists can build and maintain a loyal fanbase. The tour highlighted the value of surprise elements, personalization, and community-building rituals, showing that engaging fans in meaningful ways can elevate a concert from an event to a cultural phenomenon.

Additionally, the tour's commercial success provided insights into the business of touring. Swift's strategy of diversifying revenue streams through merchandise, digital content, and brand partnerships showed future artists how to maximize the financial potential of their tours. The tour's impact on local economies and its use of dynamic ticketing models sparked discussions about the economic and ethical aspects of the concert industry, shaping conversations that will influence how tours are planned and executed in the years to come.

In sum, the Eras Tour left an indelible mark on the music industry and popular culture. Its legacy lies in its ability to combine artistry, advocacy, fan engagement, and business acumen into a comprehensive model that redefined the concert experience. As future artists take to the stage, the influence of the Eras Tour will be evident in how they craft their performances, connect with their audiences, and navigate the complexities of the entertainment industry.

CHAPTER 8: CLOSING THE CURTAIN – REFLECTING ON THE ERAS TOUR'S LEGACY

Final Bow – The Tour's Emotional Conclusion

The final concert of the Eras Tour was a poignant, emotional event that marked the end of a journey filled with music, memories, and transformation. For both Taylor Swift and her fans, this concert was more than just a performance; it was a culmination of a multi-era celebration that had spanned months and touched millions. As the last notes of the closing song resonated through the stadium, there was a palpable mixture of joy, nostalgia, and bittersweetness in the air.

Swift, ever the consummate storyteller, made sure that the final show captured the essence of each era while also adding moments of farewell. She opened the concert with a high-energy performance that set the tone for an unforgettable night. Throughout the show, Swift paused to share stories, thank her team, and express her gratitude to the fans who had supported her through every phase of her career. These heartfelt speeches heightened the emotional weight of the evening, turning it into a communal experience of reflection and appreciation.

As the concert approached its conclusion, the atmosphere became increasingly charged. Swift's final performance was a medley that celebrated her entire career, seamlessly blending songs from her early country days to her latest indie-folk hits. The stage lit up with fireworks and confetti, creating a dazzling backdrop for Swift's last bow. With tears in her eyes, Swift stood before the crowd, taking in the overwhelming applause and love. Her final words to the audience captured the essence of the tour: a celebration of growth, change, and the enduring bond between artist and fan.

For fans, the final concert was both a joyful celebration and a somber farewell. Many had traveled great distances to be there, knowing it would be a once-in-a-lifetime experience. As they left the stadium, there was a sense of closure and the knowledge that they had been part of something truly special. The end of the Eras Tour marked the closing of a chapter, but it also hinted at new beginnings, leaving fans with anticipation for what Swift would do next.

Fan and Critical Reception – Reviews and Reflections

The fan and critical reception of the Eras Tour was overwhelmingly positive, with both groups recognizing it as a defining moment in Taylor Swift's career. Fans took to social media to share their experiences, recounting their favorite moments, surprise songs, and interactions with fellow Swifties. The tour was praised for its production value, setlist, and narrative structure, with many fans describing it as the most immersive and emotionally resonant concert they had ever attended.

Critics echoed these sentiments, lauding Swift's ability to craft a concert experience that was both grand in scale and deeply personal. Reviews highlighted the tour's ambitious production, with its elaborate stage designs, costume changes, and visual effects. Swift's performance was described as magnetic, showcasing her vocal prowess, stage presence, and storytelling skills. Critics also noted how the tour's narrative structure set a new standard for live performances, transforming the concert into a journey through

Swift's musical evolution.

While the reception was largely positive, there were areas of debate. Some critics pointed out the challenges related to ticket pricing and availability, questioning the fairness of dynamic pricing models and the difficulties many fans faced in securing tickets. These discussions, however, did not overshadow the overall acclaim for the tour. Fans and critics alike recognized that the Eras Tour was a landmark event that redefined what a concert could be, blending music, storytelling, and spectacle in a way that resonated across generations.

The fan response was particularly noteworthy for its depth of emotion. Many fans expressed how the tour had provided them with a sense of community and connection, not only to Swift but also to one another. The concert became a space where fans could relive their personal histories through Swift's songs, reflecting on how her music had been a soundtrack to their lives. This emotional resonance was a testament to the tour's impact, solidifying its place in the hearts of those who experienced it.

The Aftermath – What's Next for Swift and Her Fans

As the curtain closed on the final night of the Eras Tour, fans and industry insiders alike began to speculate on what the future held for Taylor Swift. The tour had been a monumental success, cementing Swift's status as one of the most influential and dynamic artists of her generation. It left fans wondering what Swift's next artistic direction would be and how she would build upon the legacy of the Eras Tour.

In the immediate aftermath, Swift took a moment to rest and reflect. She expressed gratitude to her fans through social media, sharing heartfelt messages and highlighting the importance of the community that had grown around her music. Swift's team also hinted at the possibility of releasing official tour footage, allowing fans to relive the experience and providing those who couldn't attend with a window into the concert's magic.

For the Swifties, the end of the tour was bittersweet. Many shared their post-tour reflections online, discussing how the Eras Tour had become a significant part of their lives and expressing a longing for the sense of unity they had felt during the concerts. However, there was also a sense of anticipation for Swift's next project. Fans speculated about potential new music, drawing on clues from Swift's past comments and her penchant for surprising her audience. The tour's conclusion did not mark the end of their journey with Swift; rather, it set the stage for the next chapter in their shared story.

The aftermath of the Eras Tour also left a lasting impression on the music industry. It raised questions about the future of concert tours, particularly in terms of scale, storytelling, and fan engagement. Swift had shown that concerts could be more than promotional events; they could be transformative experiences that blend art, commerce, and community. As fans and artists alike looked ahead, the influence of the Eras Tour on future projects was unmistakable, suggesting that its legacy would shape the direction of live music for years to come.

The Eras Tour's Place in History

The Eras Tour secured its place in music history

as one of the most ambitious, innovative, and culturally significant concert tours of all time. By spanning multiple eras of Taylor Swift's career, the tour captured the essence of her artistic journey and showcased her evolution in a way that had never been done before. Its scale, storytelling, and fan engagement set new benchmarks for the music industry, establishing it as a touchstone for future artists and concert productions.

The tour's historical significance lay in its ability to transcend the boundaries of a typical concert. It wasn't just a performance; it was an exploration of identity, growth, and the power of music to connect people across different stages of life. Swift used the tour to reflect on her past, celebrate her present, and hint at her future, creating a narrative that resonated with fans on both a personal and cultural level. This narrative approach elevated the tour into an artistic statement, solidifying Swift's reputation as a musician who could turn her personal evolution into a universal experience.

Moreover, the Eras Tour's impact on the concert industry was profound. It redefined the expectations for live performances, showing that tours could be immersive, thematic experiences that incorporated elements of theater, fashion, and visual art. The tour's success also influenced discussions about ticketing practices, fan engagement strategies, and the use of social media in building concert experiences. Its legacy, therefore, extends beyond Swift's own career, offering a blueprint for artists and producers who seek to create meaningful, multi-dimensional live shows.

In the years to come, the Eras Tour will likely be remembered as a defining moment in music history, a testament to Taylor Swift's artistry and her ability to connect with audiences on a profound level. Its influence will be felt in future concerts, inspiring artists to explore new ways of telling their stories and engaging with their fans.

Swift's Message – A Celebration of Growth and Change

At its core, the Eras Tour was a celebration of growth, change, and self-acceptance. Taylor Swift used the tour to embrace every phase of her journey, from the innocence of her early country days to the bold experimentation of her more recent albums. By presenting each era as a vital part of her evolution, Swift conveyed a powerful message: that growth is not linear, and every experience, both the highs and the lows, shapes who we become.

Throughout the tour, Swift emphasized the importance of embracing one's own story. Her performances, speeches, and interactions with fans were imbued with a sense of authenticity and vulnerability, encouraging audiences to accept their own changes and transformations. This message resonated deeply with fans, many of whom saw their own lives reflected in Swift's music and narrative. The tour became a space for celebrating not just Swift's evolution, but the growth of every person in the audience.

In closing the Eras Tour, Swift left her fans with a sense of hope and empowerment. She demonstrated that change is something to be embraced, not feared, and that each era of life carries its own beauty and significance. This overarching message of growth and self-celebration was the true legacy of the tour, leaving fans with a lasting reminder of the power of music to inspire, heal, and unite.

As the lights dimmed on the final concert, and the last echoes of applause faded, the Eras Tour's impact lingered. It was a journey that had brought people together, challenged norms, and celebrated the art of transformation. In the end, the Eras Tour was not just about Taylor Swift; it was about all of us, and the eras that define our lives.

CONCLUSION

The Eras Tour was a triumph in every sense — musically, culturally, and commercially. It stood as a testament to Taylor Swift's evolution as an artist, showcasing her remarkable ability to connect with audiences on both an intimate and grand scale. More than just a concert series, the tour was a journey through time, celebrating the different stages of Swift's career and the countless lives her music has touched along the way.

By spanning her various eras, Swift created a concert experience that was as much about self-reflection as it was about music. Each performance, costume change, and set design was meticulously crafted to tell the story of her evolution, inviting fans to witness not just her artistic growth, but also to reflect on their own journeys. In doing so, Swift transformed the concert into a shared space of nostalgia, joy, and empowerment.

The impact of the Eras Tour went far beyond the venues that hosted it. It became a cultural phenomenon, influencing fashion, social media trends, and conversations around topics such as mental health and equality. Swift's advocacy and willingness to use her platform for social change resonated with her fans, adding another layer of depth to the tour's legacy. Swifties rallied around each other, creating a vibrant community united by their love for Swift's music and the values she championed.

Critically acclaimed and commercially groundbreaking, the Eras Tour redefined what a concert could be. It set new standards for live performances, integrating storytelling, production, and fan engagement in ways that will influence the music industry for years to come. As future artists take inspiration from the tour's narrative structure, fan inclusivity, and innovative business strategies, the legacy of the Eras Tour will continue to shape the concert landscape.

In the end, the Eras Tour was more than a retrospective of Taylor Swift's career; it was a celebration of growth, change, and the beauty of embracing one's journey. Swift used her music and the tour to remind fans that every era — whether marked by joy, heartbreak, or self-discovery — is an integral part of who we are. As the tour closes, it leaves behind a powerful message: that our stories, like Swift's, are ever-evolving, and each chapter is worth celebrating. The Eras Tour may have taken its final bow, but its influence will echo in the hearts of fans and the music world for years to come.

WANT MORE IN A NUTSHELL?

Curious for more quick, engaging reads that make complex stories simple?

The *In a Nutshell* series offers concise, entertaining overviews of pop culture, history, and trending topics—perfect for readers who love to learn, laugh, and stay informed.

Explore the full *In a Nutshell* collection and discover other books and audiobooks by **Felix Grayson**, published by **MindSpark Publishing**.

Visit **FelixGrayson.com** to see what's new,

what's trending, and what's next.

FelixGrayson.com

Big ideas don't need big books.

Sometimes, the best stories fit perfectly—in a nutshell.

ACKNOWLEDGEMENT

This book would not have been possible without the incredible support and inspiration of so many people. First and foremost, I would like to thank Taylor Swift and the Swifties worldwide for creating such a remarkable cultural phenomenon. Your passion, creativity, and dedication were the driving forces behind this journey.

A special thank you goes to those who have contributed to and documented the Eras Tour, from the production team to the media outlets that captured its magic. Your work provided the insights and stories that helped bring this book to life.

To my family, friends, and readers—thank you for your constant encouragement and belief in this project. Your support has made every step of this process rewarding. This book is a celebration of music, growth, and the power of storytelling, and I am grateful to have shared it with you.

ABOUT THE AUTHOR

Felix Grayson has always been fascinated by the stories that shape our culture—from defining historical events to the moments in pop culture that captivate millions. With a lifelong passion for storytelling and discovery, Felix brings clarity and insight to complex topics, making them accessible, engaging, and fun to explore.

As the creator of the *In a Nutshell* series, Felix combines thoughtful research with concise sto-

rytelling to deliver quick yet meaningful overviews of the people, events, and trends shaping
our world. His mission is simple: to make learning enjoyable for everyone, no matter how busy
life gets.

When he's not diving into the latest cultural
phenomenon or uncovering forgotten chapters
of history, Felix enjoys connecting with readers,
sharing ideas, and exploring new stories—one
nutshell at a time.